SPURTING ARTERIES AND FLOODING OCEANS
WHAT TO DO IN CASE OF DISASTERS GREAT AND SMALL

D0507826

JESSE GOOSSENS & LINDE FAAS

Spurting ARteries + Flooding Oceans

WHAT TO DO IN CASE OF
DISASTERS GREAT AND SMALL

TRANSLATED BY JAN WARNDORFF

LEMNISCAAT

Jesse Goossens and Linde Faas also wrote (published by Lemniscaat):

Cola Fountains and Splattering Paint Bombs

The authors thank Frank Tebbe, Cees van Romburgh, Yvonne Breedijk
and the Dutch and International Red Cross for their helpful advice.

First published in the UK in 2017 by Lemniscaat Ltd,
Kemp House, 152 City Road, London EC1V 2NX
Distributed worldwide by Thames & Hudson,
181A High Holborn, London WC1V 7QX

ISBN 13: 978-1-78807-014-0 (hardcover)
Printing and binding: Wilco, Amersfoort
First UK edition

www.lemniscaat.co.uk

MIX
Papier van
verantwoorde herkomst
FSC® C004472

CONTENTS

PREFACE BY HER ROYAL HIGHNESS PRINCESS MARGRIET OF THE NETHERLANDS

Boys and girls,

Disasters and emergencies are thankfully and usually not common to us. Neither do we think about what we should do in such a situation. But actually, we should be prepared!

I have been a volunteer for the Red Cross for a long time. The Red Cross helps people who have been affected by a disaster or an armed conflict. We have been doing so for over 150 years and for all people worldwide, no matter who or where they are. We do so by providing food, tents and blankets, for example. During these many years we have learned that you shouldn't just help after a disaster has happened, but that it's better to act beforehand. It is essential to be prepared for emergency situations in order to improve the chances of survival. And not just for yourself, but also for the people around you.

Whether it's a far-away disaster or one close to home: just imagining the measures you can take is actually quite exiting. It's all about using your knowledge, your skills and your own ideas to undertake personal action. This book offers lots of useful ideas you could consider for when it comes to disasters and how to act in response. This is not an official first-aid book, but really a book that helps you think about how you can become more resilient. There's also lots of practical stuff, like putting together emergency kits and lessons and exercises in first aid. To name just a simple thing: do you keep some bottles of water at home, in case the taps suddenly stop working?

Once you've read this book, you'll have a good general idea of what there is to know about disasters and what you can do – how you can prepare for things we all hope will never happen. So you can help yourself and others if needed. The Red Cross wants everyone to be ready for an emergency situation.

You too can do something!

PRINCESS OF THE NETHERLANDS
Honorary Chair of The Netherlands Red Cross

THE 4 BASIC RULES

Disasters come in many shapes and sizes, but there are 4 rules that apply in each and every case. So knowing these 4 rules by heart is a good first step in learning how to respond.

Important: always check whether there are any adults around who can help. Don't do anything unless there is no other help available.

1. Focus on safety
Check whether you are in any danger. If you are, get yourself to safety.

Are other people in danger? Let them know, and help them if necessary.

Is the victim in danger? If so, get him to safety. If there is no immediate danger, don't move him – you don't yet know what is wrong with him, and moving him could make it worse.

2. Check what happened and what is the matter with the victim
First, see if you can figure out what went wrong. You can sometimes tell this from the environment, or objects lying near the victim.

After that – not before – you should check to see what is the matter with the victim: you need to know what happened in order to give him the help he needs.

3. Call the emergency telephone number if necessary
With accidents on the street, always call the emergency telephone number. Shout for help as soon as you see that a victim needs help. If there are no adults around, call the emergency telephone number yourself.

Determine what's needed right away: ambulance, fire brigade, police... The people of the emergency call service can help you best if you explain the situation clearly and calmly.

4. Assist the victim
Even if you can't move the victim, you can still for example put a blanket over him to keep him warm, hold an umbrella over him if it's raining, or shelter him from the wind.

Download the Red Cross's first aid app. You also need the rest of this book, because the help you need to give is different for each disaster.

Good luck!

PS. Disasters can happen to anyone – it doesn't matter if you're young or old, short or tall, where you were born or whether you're a boy or a girl. Still, in this book, victims are always referred to as "he". That's just because it's easier that way.

DISASTERS

in and around

the house

RESUSCITATION

When serious disasters happen, you may need to be able to resuscitate someone. If there are no adults nearby, always call the emergency telephone number first if someone has lost consciousness and does not respond when you talk to him or shake him.

If the victim stops breathing, you can try to resuscitate him until the ambulance arrives.

1   Put the victim on his back.
2   Make sure the victim's airway is unobstructed by carefully tilting his head back and using 2 fingers to lift his chin (this is called a chin lift).
3   Watch and listen for 10 seconds: can you hear or see the victim breathing? No? In that case, begin with chest compressions.
    - Kneel down next to the victim's chest.
    - Place the heel of your hand on the middle of his chest.
    - Place the heel of your other hand on your first hand.
    - Twine your fingers together and make sure that they're not touching the victim's chest.
    - Straighten your arms and make sure that your shoulders are directly above your hands.
    - Press the victim's sternum (breastbone) straight down, 5 to 6 centimetres.
    - Allow the victim's sternum to spring back all the way, but don't take your hands off his chest.

4   Do this 30 times – about 2 times per second.
5   Perform the chin lift and tilt the victim's head back.
6   Give the victim mouth-to-mouth resuscitation:
    - Blow your breath into his mouth for 1 second.
    - Check to see if his chest rises when you do so.
    - Let him breathe out.
7   Do it once again.
8   Keep repeating this: 30 chest compressions, 2 mouth-to-mouth breaths.

MAKING A FIRST-AID KIT

Make sure you always have a first-aid kit with you. Put it in an easy-to-reach place in the house, put one in your parents' car and be sure to always bring one with you when you go on holiday.

This kit should contain (standard contents for 2 adults and 2 children):

- medication that your family members absolutely need
- telephone numbers of your family doctor and emergency services
- a packet of 25 adhesive bandages in various sizes
- a role of adhesive tape
- 2 rolls of bandages
- 2 rolls of elastic bandages
- 5 sterile gauzes measuring 5 x 5 cm
- 5 sterile gauzes measuring 10 x 10 cm
- a bottle of disinfectant
- a piece of cloth for giving mouth-to-mouth resuscitation
- a pair of tick tweezers
- a pair of scissors
- tweezers
- a thermometer (not quicksilver)
- a packet of paracetamol
- 2 pairs of latex disposable gloves
- a flashlight with new batteries
- optionally: a rescue blanket (one of those thin ones that is very warm)

Cloth for Mouth to Mouth Resuscitation

Medication

important phone numbers

Rescue blanket

paracetamol

Scissors

thermometer

adhesive tape

bandages

elastic bandages

adhesive bandages

Flashlight

latex disposable gloves

tick tweezers

batteries

(5cm)

(10cm)

Sterile gauzes

tweezers

BROKEN BONES

REMARKABLE Robert Craig "Evel" Knievel was an American stunt performer. He especially gained fame with his motorcycle jumps over great distances and peculiar objects, such as a 6 metre-long crate full of rattlesnakes, 2 mountain lions, 14 buses, a ravine, a huge fountain in Las Vegas...

His last 2 jumps went badly – and they were not the only ones. Evel Knievel suffered 433 broken bones throughout his life, involving from 35 different bones – from his skull, nose and all his ribs to his hips, back, wrists, ankles and toes. He even made the *Guinness Book of World Records*.

Luckily, though, he survived all of his stunts. When he eventually died, it was of lung disease.

DID YOU KNOW?

- Falls are the most common kind of accidents. And falling can be enough to break a bone, of course.
- There are 5 types of bone fractures:
    1. TRANSVERSE FRACTURES: the bone breaks straight across.
    2. MULTIPLE FRACTURES: the bone breaks in several places.
    3. OBLIQUE FRACTURES: the bone breaks diagonally.
    4. SPIRAL FRACTURES: the bone was twisted until it broke.
    5. GREENSTICK FRACTURES: the bone is broken, but the periosteum (the membrane that covers the bone) is still whole.

- Adults have approximately 206 bones in their bodies. Babies are born with up to 350 bones, but some of those fuse together afterwards.
- The 5 bones that break most often are the humerus (the bone in your upper arm), the radius (the bone in your lower arm on the side of your thumb), the ulna (the other bone in your lower arm), the tibia (the shinbone) and the fibula (the calf bone).
- The most painful bone to break is your femur (thigh bone).

WHAT TO DO

- Do not move the victim and make sure he moves as little as possible.
- Call for help.
- If he has injured his back, hip, leg or knee, **call the emergency telephone number.**
- If the broken body part is very pale or blue, **call the emergency telephone number.**
- If the victim is in a lot of pain or has an open fracture (you can see the bone), **call the emergency telephone number.**
- If the victim has a broken leg, support it with your hand or a blanket.
- If the victim has broken his arm or shoulder, have him support his arm himself.
- Do not try to straighten or bend broken bones.

BLOOD

REMARKABLE If the largest artery in your body – the abdominal aorta – is cut, you can bleed to death in 20 seconds. With other large arteries, it can take 2 to 3 minutes, if you don't get any help.

Until the nineteenth century, "bloodletting" was a standard treatment for diseases. Blood was removed from the body by making small cuts or placing leeches on the patient's body, the idea being that this would balance and purify the body. This was also performed on the American president George Washington when he woke up one morning at the age of 67 and found that he had trouble breathing. 3 doctors gave him bloodlettings, together draining him of more than half of his blood. It didn't help. Washington died – most likely due to shock from having insufficient blood.

DID YOU KNOW?

- Without blood, we can't live. Blood transports oxygen and nutrients to all the cells in your body and removes all the waste.
- Adults have over 100,000 kilometres of blood vessels in their bodies. That's enough to go around the world 2.5 times.
- It takes between 2 0seconds and 1 minute for a drop of blood to leave your heart, go around your entire body, and come back to the heart again.
- Your body produces 17 million red blood cells per second – and it can make up to 7 times more than that if necessary!
- Blood makes up 8 per cent of your body weight. A child weighing 40 kilos has about 2 litres of blood.
- Your blood contains real gold. A tiny amount – in an adult, it's just 0.2 milligrams. But still!

WHAT TO DO

- Is the victim bleeding a lot? **Call the emergency telephone number.**
- You can clean small wounds with water (e.g. from the tap). Don't try to clean large wounds yourself.
- If there is a lot of blood, take a folded piece of clean cloth or bandage and press it hard against the wound. Keep pressing. If there is no cloth available, just use your hand, or get the victim to hold the wound closed himself.
- Put the victim down and cover him with a blanket if necessary.
- If you get another person's blood on you, wash yourself as soon as the emergency is over.
- Always go to the doctor if someone has a deep wound, has been bitten by an animal, there is something in the wound that won't come out or if the wound won't stop bleeding.

BURNS

REMARKABLE In the past, people were sometimes punished by being burned alive at the stake, for instance if people thought you were a witch, if you had committed treason or didn't have the right religion. Jeanne d'Arc is probably the most famous victim of this punishment.

You might hope that that doesn't happen anymore today, but in Bangladesh, India and Pakistan, thousands of women are still soaked with kerosene or another kind of fuel and set aflame each year. Why? Because they couldn't pay their dowry, or because they're not getting pregnant fast enough. As for the police, they just get told that it was an accident in the kitchen...

DID YOU KNOW?

- Burns cause almost the worst pain a person can feel.
- Burns are third in the list of most deadly accidents.
- There are 3 "degrees" of burns:
  1. FIRST DEGREE BURNS: the skin is not broken; red or pink in colour; dry and painful.
  2. SECOND DEGREE BURNS: the skin is still flexible, but broken; red, pink or white in colour; wet and painful; blisters.
  3. THIRD DEGREE BURNS: the skin is stiff and severely damaged; white or beige to dark brown in colour; dry; barely hurts.
- 44 per cent of burns is bad enough for people to seek medical help are caused by fire: gas flames, cigarettes or fireworks, for instance. Gas flames and candle flames are very hot: about 1,000 degrees Celsius.
- 33 per cent is caused by hot liquids or steam. This is the most common type of burn suffered by children.
- 23 per cent is caused by other things, such as chemical liquids, electricity or the sun. People often get sunburned, but that is usually just a first-degree burn – it doesn't need a doctor.

WHAT TO DO

- Water first, everything else can wait! Cool the burned area with lukewarm (not cold), running water for 10 to 20 minutes.
- Remove clothing and jewellery if they are not stuck to the wound.
- Cover severe burns with sterile gauze, clean cloth or clean plastic (shrink wrap).
- You can take care of light (first degree) burns yourself. For large burns, contact your family doctor.

IMMEDIATELY CALL THE EMERGENCY TELEPHONE NUMBER IF:

- a large part of the body is burned (second or third degree).
- the burns are on the face, ears, hands, feet, joints or genitalia.
- the burns go all the way around the neck, a limb or the torso.
- the burns are located in the airways.

BITES AND STINGS

REMARKABLE Bill Haast was fascinated by snakes from a very young age, and paid for it: he was bitten by a rattlesnake and a copperhead when he was just 12. But he was to suffer, and survive, another 170 snake bites; many of which would have been lethal for other people. He became the director of the Miami Serpentarium and began to milk snakes: their venom is used to make anti-venom and medicines. In order to make himself immune, Bill injected himself with diluted snake venom every week.

Bill Haast lived to be 100.

WHAT TO DO

- If someone who has been bitten or stung begins to vomit, has significant stomach pains, or if his lips or throat begin to swell, he has trouble breathing or goes into shock, **immediately call the emergency telephone number.**
- Ask if they're allergic and have an EpiPen on them – they can inject themselves with that.
- If the stinger is still in the victim's body, lever it out with a flat object, such as a bank card.
- If necessary, use an anti-itch cream. You can also cool the sting with a cold washcloth.
- If the area around the sting swells up a lot, call your family doctor. If the victim has been stung in the mouth or throat, have him suck an ice cube to reduce the swelling.
- If there is a tick on the person's body, use a pair of tick tweezers or get a pair of regular tweezers and grab the tick by the head, as close to the skin as possible, and pull straight up from the skin.
- Wash the sting or bite with soap and water.
- If the bite is deep (e.g. from a dog), always seek medical help.

- In case of a bite from a venomous snake or another venomous animal, **always call the emergency telephone number.** If you know what kind of snake it was, make sure you tell them that!
- Keep the victim calm. That way, the venom spreads more slowly.
- Press a clean cloth on the wound until it stops bleeding.
- Never try to suck the venom out of a wound – that could put you in danger.

DID YOU KNOW?

The top 3 of most painful bites and stings is:

3 THE STONEFISH: it looks like a stone, but woe to you if you step on it! The excruciating pain can persist for days or even longer, and is so bad that some people beg to have their foot amputated.

2 THE BULLET ANT: the largest ant in the world, which is called the bullet ant because its sting feels like being shot.

1 THE BOX JELLYFISH: they come in all shapes and sizes, and have the most powerful venom in the animal kingdom. Many people who are stung by them go into shock and drown as a result.

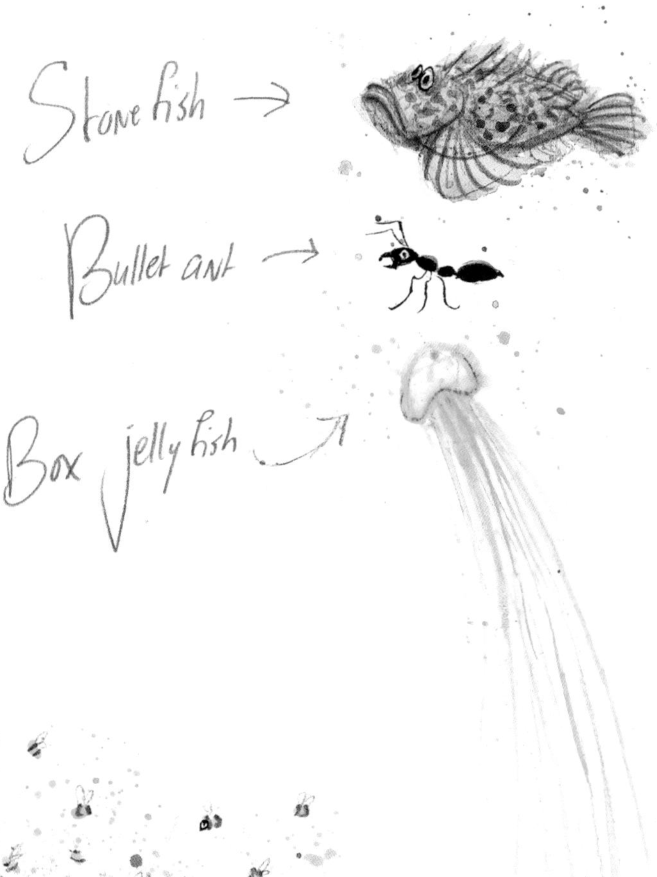

Stone fish →

Bullet ant →

Box jellyfish ↗

CHOKING

REMARKABLE During the time of the Romans, it was not uncommon for people to vomit on purpose during banquets, so that they could eat more. Emperor Claudius did it too: he used a feather to tickle his uvula, at the back of his throat, to make himself throw up. There are historians who believe that this eventually killed him – in the year 54, he allegedly swallowed his feather and choked on it. (But there are also people who say that he was poisoned by his wife).

DID YOU KNOW?

- People are the only creatures who can choke on their food – we are the only mammal that cannot breathe and swallow at the same time.
- You swallow about 600 times per day. Each swallow uses 26 different muscles.
- On average, 100 people die each year from choking on a ballpoint pen.
- 80 per cent of all emergency phone calls about choking concerns children under 6 years old.
- Round things are the most dangerous, because they close off your windpipe completely: cherry tomatoes, nuts, grapes, hard candies, coins and buttons, for instance.
- Toothpicks are also dangerous: each year, 9,000 emergencies occur because someone swallowed a toothpick.
- A child who cannot breathe suffocates in 4 to 6 minutes, and adults in 10.

WHAT TO DO

- Can the person still cough and breathe? Then let him cough, and don't do anything.
- If he cannot talk, cough or breathe, **call the emergency telephone number** and put your phone in speaker mode.
- Hit the patient on the back 5 times: hit them hard between the shoulder blades with the flat of your hand. See if the object comes out of their throat. If not, give them 5 stomach blows, called the Heimlich manoeuvre:
  - Stand behind the victim and place one of your legs between his legs.
  - Circle your arms around his stomach.
  - Place the thumb of your fist just above his belly button.
  - Grab your fist with your other hand and pull your fist inwards and upwards into the victim's stomach, as hard as you can.
  - Keep doing this in quick succession until the object comes out of the victim's throat or help arrives.
- If the victim loses consciousness, begin resuscitation (see p. 12).

NEAR-DROWNING

REMARKABLE Towards the end of the Second World War, when Germany was losing against Russia, the German army decided to evacuate a large number of people because the Red Army was on the way. The military transport ship Wilhelm Gustloff was to take aboard 6,050 refugees and wounded German soldiers at a port in East Poland and bring them to safety. The plan was called "Operation Hannibal".

A lot more people boarded the ship than were on the passenger list: 10,582 in all. And the ship did not make it far – after just a few dozen kilometres, the ship was spotted by a Russian submarine and hit with 3 torpedoes.

1,252 of the people on board were saved, but 9,343 people were swallowed by the icy waters of the Baltic Sea. Among them were over 5,000 children.

DID YOU KNOW?

- 1.2 million people drown each year: that's 1 death every 26 seconds.
- Drowning is the primary cause of death among children between the age of 0 and 5. More people also die between the age of 20 and 25 (probably because they are more involved with water sports and because they are more reckless) and over the age of 65.
- The largest number of people drown at the end of the afternoon. It's the hottest part of the day, when people start to get tired.
- A quarter of all drownings happens in water that is less than 1 metre deep. And 40 per cent of the people who drown does so within 2 metres of the coast or the edge of the swimming pool.
- Once underwater and unable to come up for air, a person dies within 3 to 5 minutes.

WHAT TO DO

Someone in distress in the water usually doesn't call for help, because he needs all his strength just to gasp for air. If you see someone who keeps disappearing under the water, trying to swim but not making any progress, and of course if he is calling for help, take immediate action.

- **Call for help from the lifeguards or call the emergency telephone number.**
- Throw something to the victim that he can hold on to.
- Do not do anything that could get you into trouble too: never go into the water without a form of safety.
- Once the drowning person is out of the water, put him on his back and talk to him.
- If he is breathing normally, roll him onto his side and put a blanket over him.
- If he is not breathing, begin resuscitating him immediately (see p. 12) until the ambulance arrives.
- Even if the victim seems to be doing well, he still needs to see a doctor. If there is water in his lungs, this can still cause major problems hours later.

POISONING

REMARKABLE Cyanide is the poison that has caused most deaths worldwide. It is a component of the infamous Zyklon B, which was used to kill people in the gas chambers of the Second World War. It is also common in murder stories: if you can smell bitter almonds near a corps, that's your smoking gun right there. It's just that only 4 in 10 people can actually smell it.

Cyanide can also be found in apricot kernels: the kernel you find when you break open the stone in an apricot. Eating just 3 of those little kernels puts you at risk of death.

DID YOU KNOW?

- There are 5 ways for poison or venom to enter your body:
  1. swallowing it;
  2. breathing it in;
  3. through the eyes;
  4. through the skin;
  5. through a bite or sting.
- Nearly half of all poisonings happens to children under the age of 6. The substances in question are cosmetics, cleaning agents and painkillers.
- 90 per cent of all poisonings happens at home.
- When you're poisoned, you won't always realise it right away. Our bodies react within seconds to some poisons, but with others it can take hours or even days.
- The fugu fish is a delicacy in Japan – and deadly if it's not prepared correctly. The poison in just 1 fish is enough to kill 30 people.
- Worldwide, 351,000 people die of food poisoning every year, and 193,500 of other kinds of poisoning. And there are also people who take poison on purpose. 370,000 people die each year after swallowing pesticides, for example.

WHAT TO DO

- If you or someone else loses consciousness, feels anxious and short of breath, feels lethargic or has extensive wounds: make sure of your own safety and call or have someone **call the emergency telephone number.**
- In all other cases, call your family doctor.
- If someone has swallowed something poisonous, do NOT make him vomit. Immediately have him rinse his mouth with water and spit it out.
- If someone has poison on his skin, take off the clothes that have poison on them and rinse the skin with lots of water (preferably lukewarm) until professional help can take over.
- If someone has breathed poison, take him somewhere where there is fresh air. Begin resuscitating him (see p. 12) if he stops responding when you talk to him or shake his shoulder.
- If poison has got into someone's eyes, rinse the eye with running water for ten minutes, from the inner corner of the eye to the outer.

FAINTING

REMARKABLE Fainting won't kill you – but sometimes, people faint as a result of another problem, for instance a stroke. And things can go wrong in other ways as well.

Dawn McGookin wasn't feeling well, so she went to get a glass of water to sip from. As she walked back with the glass in her hands, she fainted and fell on top of the glass, which broke. The shards of the glass cut her arteries, and she bled out and died on the spot.

DID YOU KNOW?

- If your brain does not get any oxygen for 8 to 10 seconds, you lose consciousness.
- Women faint much more often than men. Among other reasons, they have less blood in their bodies than men, so it is easier for their brains not to get enough blood/oxygen.
- 20 to 30 per cent of cases where someone faints is due to a heart problem, but 50 per cent is never explained.
- In the nineteenth century, women fainted all the time. Mostly because of their corsets, which were much too tight.
- Ever since Elvis Presley and The Beatles, tons of people – especially girls – faint at pop concerts. The cause: overheating, dehydration and pure excitement.
- Nearly 15 per cent of all people (almost) faints when they see blood.
- The largest percentage of people who faint are older people who, for example, sit up or stand up too quickly, causing a sudden drop in their blood pressure.

WHAT TO DO

WHEN SOMEONE HAS FAINTED:

- Put him on his side.
- Loosen any tight clothing.
- Give him space. So don't crowd in close around him with a lot of people.
- If he doesn't come to soon, **call the emergency telephone number.**

HEATSTROKE

REMARKABLE Each year, dozens of children die of heatstroke because their parents left them in a car while they went shopping or something – and forgot that their child was still in the back seat. In the United States alone, there are 40 such deaths every year. 70 per cent of those deaths are children under the age of 2.

In 10 minutes, the temperature in a car can rise by 10 degrees Celsius – it doesn't matter if the windows are open or closed. Even if the temperature outside is 15 degrees Celsius, the temperature in a car in direct sunlight can climb as high as 40 degrees Celsius. Imagine how bad that can get in the summer!

You can suffer heatstroke at 40 degrees and up, and if your body temperature rises above 42 degrees Celsius, you may die. Heatstroke is the primary cause of deaths in cars – aside from accidents – among children under the age of 14.

With animals, it's even more common – hundreds of pets die from heat every year because their owners left them in a car.

DID YOU KNOW?

- Among teens and young adults, sunstroke is one of the primary causes of death. It happens most often when they are playing sports in the sun.
- There are 3 stages to suffering a heatstroke:
  1. HEAT CRAMPS: muscle aches and cramps in the stomach and legs.
  2. HEAT EXHAUSTION: the skin is cool and clammy to the touch and looks pale, grey or red. The victim has a headache, is nauseous and feels dizzy and weak and tired.
  3. HEATSTROKE: extremely high body temperature; dry or clammy red skin; quick, weak pulse; quick, shallow breathing. The victim is confused, may lose consciousness from time to time, vomits and may have seizures.

WHAT TO DO

HEAT CRAMPS:

- Bring the victim to a cool place.
- Let him sit or lie down in a relaxing way and massage the spots that hurt.
- Don't let him drink water or any other drink that is too cold.

HEAT EXHAUSTION:

- Bring the victim to a cooler place, preferably somewhere ventilated, and make him lie down.
- Protect him from the sun.
- Don't let him drink water or any other drink that is too cold.
- If the victim doesn't want to drink, loses consciousness or begins to vomit, **call the emergency telephone number.**

HEATSTROKE:

- **Call the emergency telephone number immediately.**
- Lie the victim down in a cool environment.
- Don't let him exert himself.
- Don't let him eat or drink anything.
- Cool the victim down as well as you can. Use cold packs or towels soaked in cold water that you replace when they get warmer – but make sure that he doesn't start to shiver. Continue doing this until the patient's condition improves or help arrives.

HYPOTHERMIA

REMARKABLE The Norwegian doctor Anna Bågenholm was skiing when she had a strange fall: at a waterfall, she fell into the water and became stuck between the ice and the rocks. Her friends grabbed her feet and called the emergency services.

Anna managed to find a pocket of air and continued to move for 40 minutes. It took 80 minutes before the emergency services arrived. By that time, she wasn't moving anymore, had no pulse, and her circulation had stopped. In the hospital, she was connected to a heart machine and her blood was slowly warmed up. 100 doctors worked for 9 hours to save her life.

Luckily, Anna regained consciousness. She can't use her hands properly anymore, but she is back to working part-time – and she is skiing again.

DID YOU KNOW?

- You become hypothermic if your body temperature drops to 35 degrees Celsius or lower. If your temperature drops below 30 degrees Celsius, you lose consciousness. Under 25 degrees Celsius, your blood stops circulating and you die.
- 28,000 people die of hypothermia each year. Most of these victims are older people, who cannot shiver very well – and shivering warms you up.
- Men become hypothermic more easily than women.
- You become hypothermic much more quickly in cold water than in cold air: your temperature drops 25 times faster in water. Because of that, you can become hypothermic in the rain, even if the temperature is not below freezing.
- Sometimes, when they grow hypothermic, people get the strange impulse to take off their clothes.
- When using alcohol or drugs, you get hypothermia more easily, because your veins become wider.

WHAT TO DO

When someone becomes hypothermic, they become confused or sleepy, start talking slowly, have a weak pulse and shiver intensely – or, instead, can't move well anymore.

- **Call the emergency telephone number** if the victim is lethargic or loses consciousness.
- If possible, bring the victim to a warm place.
- Wrap the victim in blankets.
- If he can still drink, give him something warm to drink, but no alcohol.
- If parts of his body are frozen (e.g. fingers or toes), don't rub them warm, but wrap them thickly in warm cloth or hold them in your armpit, for example, to warm them up.

SHOCK

REMARKABLE The body's reaction to sudden loss of blood or fluids is called "shock". Allergic reactions, too, can cause shock symptoms. When suddenly losing blood or fluids, the body attempts to limit the consequences of the loss: the heart beats faster to circulate the remaining blood to the organs that are necessary for survival: the heart, the lungs and the brains. Breathing becomes more rapid, too. It is said sometimes that it is possible to go into shock when hearing news that affects you very strongly, positively or negatively, but as to whether that is true...

In India, 470 people died of "shock" – according to official reports – when they heard that Ms Jayalalithaa, Chief Minister of the state of Tamil Nadu, had passed away. The bereaved of these shock casualties all received 300,000 rupees from Jayalalithaa's political party (the average monthly salary in India is 18,120 rupees).

DID YOU KNOW?

- People go into shock when their blood pressure suddenly decreases very quickly. This means that their cells no longer receive enough blood, as a result of which they gradually start to die off.
- 1 in 5 people who go into shock dies as a result.
- It is not clear exactly how many people die of shock each year, because shock ultimately causes heart failure, which is then usually listed as the cause of death.
- Shock can be caused in various ways, such as:
  - major blood loss;
  - severe burns;
  - certain bacteria;
  - severe allergic reactions;
  - heart failure;
  - dehydration.
- If shock is not treated, it is almost always deadly.

WHAT TO DO

When someone goes into shock, the colour drains from his face, he begins to breathe quickly and shallowly, has a rapid pulse and dilated pupils, and he may lose consciousness.

- Shock is life-threatening. Always **call the emergency telephone number.**
- Lie the victim down.
- If he is bleeding, press the wound closed.
- Loosen any tight clothing and put a blanket over the victim if necessary.
- If the victim begins to vomit, roll him onto his side so that he doesn't choke.
- If the victim stops breathing, begin resuscitation (see p. 12).

HEART FAILURE

REMARKABLE There is such a thing as a happy heart syndrome: people whose heart fails spontaneously when something very special happens – their favourite football club wins a cup, a particularly festive birthday party, or something similar.

The first known example of this is Diagoras of Rhodos, a famous boxer who lived during the fifth century B.C. After a successful career, he saw his 2 sons win at the Olympic Games of 448 B.C. His sons hoisted him onto their shoulders and carried him through the stadium, full of cheering spectators. Diagoras died of happiness on the spot. There is a football club named after him on Rhodos: Diagoras FC.

DID YOU KNOW?

- Cardiovascular diseases are the leading cause of death worldwide: 17.3 million people die of it every year.
- Often what we call a heart failure is actually the heart "fibrillating": the pumping function of the heart has failed, and its pulse has gone haywire. The blood is no longer circulating and the organs aren't getting any oxygen. After 10 minutes of fibrillation, the heart usually fails completely.
- A defibrillator (an AED) can help bring the heart's pulse back to normal. It does not help if the heart has truly stopped.
- The most common cause for heart failure is heart disease.
- During heart failure, brain cells become irreparably damaged due to lack of oxygen after just 4 to 6 minutes.
- Every minute that someone goes without help reduces his chances of survival by 7 to 10 per cent.
- X-ray research on mummies shows that heart failures were already common in ancient Egypt.

WHAT TO DO

- If someone has stopped breathing, or is breathing very shallowly and no longer responds, even when you shake him, **immediately call the emergency telephone number**
- Begin resuscitation (see p. 12).
- Ask if anyone can find and use a defibrillator (AED) until the ambulance arrives. As long as the heart is fibrillating, you can use an AED.

HEART ATTACK

REMARKABLE Tommy Cooper was a famous magician. Or rather, he was a magician whose tricks always failed, and eventually he turned that into his act – although he would have preferred to really be a good magician.

On 15 April 1984, he performed live on the English television programme *Live from Her Majesty's*. When, in the middle of his act, he suddenly gasped for air and fell down, everyone thought it was just another joke: the audience laughed uproariously. Even his assistant laughed, because he thought Tommy was improvising. It took a while before people realised that he was having a heart attack. When they did, the orchestra was signalled to play the theme leading up to advertisements and Tommy was pulled behind the curtains.

They tried to resuscitate Tommy backstage, but it was to no avail. By the time Tommy reached the hospital, he was declared dead.

DID YOU KNOW?

- When suffering a heart attack, part of the heart no longer gets any blood because one of the coronary arteries is blocked.
- A heart attack can cause heart failure.
- People who live alone are twice as likely to suffer a heart attack than people who live together with someone else.
- People who laugh a lot are less likely to have a heart attack. Depression and gloominess, on the other hand, can increase the odds.
- 40 per cent of people who have a heart attack dies before they get to the hospital.
- Heart attacks are most common on Mondays. Christmas Day and Boxing Day also have increased heart attack rates.
- About 25 per cent of all heart attacks passes without being noticed and are only discovered during later examinations.

- Women who smoke are at risk of a heart attack 19 years before women who do not.

WHAT TO DO

If someone experiences a tight pain in the middle of their chest, which may radiate to the upper arms, jaw, back and stomach, for more than 5 minutes, here is what you must do:

- **Call the emergency telephone number.**
- Have the victim sit down in a chair or with his back against a wall.
- Keep talking to and reassuring him until the ambulance arrives.

STROKE

REMARKABLE People who suffer a stroke can end up with completely changed personalities.

Chris Birch was a rugby player and bank employee who was about to marry his girlfriend when he had an unusual accident: he tried to impress his friends by doing a backflip, but broke his neck and had a stroke. After his recovery he was a different person: he was no longer attracted to women, broke off his engagement and quit his job. He became a hairdresser instead, and now has a boyfriend.

DID YOU KNOW?

- About 13 million people suffer a stroke each year. It is the second leading cause of death in the world.
- People who do not smoke but live with someone who does, have a 70 per cent greater chance of suffering a stroke.
- The main causes of stroke are high blood pressure, diabetes and smoking.
- A TIA (transient ischemic attack) is a stroke that passes – half of all people who experience a TIA never even realise it.
- The odds of having a stroke depends on your descent:
  - Native Americans & Alaska Natives: 5.3 per cent
  - Afro-Americans: 3.2 per cent
  - Caucasians: 2.5 per cent
  - Asians: 2.4 per cent
- Still, most strokes occur in Indonesia, Mongolia and Russia.
- 60 per cent of people who suffer a stroke waits until the following day to see a doctor.
- 20 per cent of people who suffer a stroke dies within a month.

- Damage to the left side of the brain can cause paralysis in the right side of the body, and vice versa.

WHAT TO DO

- If someone's mouth becomes lopsided, someone speaks in a confused way or cannot move his arm, **call the emergency telephone number immediately.**
- If you're not sure:
  1. Ask the victim to bare his teeth. If his mouth is not straight, **call the emergency telephone number.**
  2. Have the victim say a simple sentence. If he can't, **call the emergency telephone number.**
  3. Have the victim stretch his arms out in front of him and turn his palms upwards. If one of his arms drops down, **call the emergency telephone number.**
- Have the victim lie down with his head on a pillow or a folded piece of cloth until the ambulance arrives.
- Do not let the victim eat or drink anything.
- If the victim loses consciousness, roll him onto his side.
- If the victim stops breathing, begin resuscitation (see p. 12).

CAR ACCIDENT

REMARKABLE In some very rare circumstances, a car crash can be a good thing. An American lorry driver, Richard Paylor, was eating an apple as he drove along the motorway when a piece of apple got stuck in his throat. He couldn't breathe, and lost consciousness.

His truck went off the road and crashed through the barriers. The force of the impact caused Richard to smack into the steering wheel with his chest, which dislodged the piece of apple from his throat. His life was saved by the accident.

DID YOU KNOW?

- Traffic accidents are the main cause of death among people between the ages of 15 and 29.
- Every year, nearly 1.3 million people die in a car accident around the world: that's 1 death every 26 seconds. A further 20 to 50 million people are injured or handicapped.
- Talking on a cell phone while driving increases the risk of an accident by 400 per cent.
- Most deadly traffic accidents take place on Saturdays. The safest days are Mondays, Tuesdays and Wednesdays.
- Most traffic accidents occur within 5 kilometres of the victim's home.
- Men cause twice as many car accidents as women.
- The most common injuries in car accidents are back and neck injuries.
- On average, each person is involved in a car accident once every 18 years.
- Most fatalities occur when the car flips over.

WHAT TO DO

IF YOU WITNESS A CAR ACCIDENT IN WHICH PEOPLE ARE INJURED:

- **Call the emergency telephone number.**
- Check that you yourself are not in danger.
- Make sure that people stand or sit behind the crash barrier if they can. Put on a safety vest if you have one.
- Do not move someone if he cannot get out of the car himself. People with neck or back pain must stay in the car.
- If several people have been injured, go to the quietest one first: he could be unconscious and in the greatest need of help.
- Use cloth (clothing) to stem the flow of blood from wounds.
- If necessary, use what you have learned in the "Broken bones", "Blood", "Fainting" and "Shock" sections of this book until the ambulance arrives.

Major DISASTERS

BEFORE AND AFTER DISASTER

To make sure that you can respond well when a disaster occurs, you can make the following preparations:

- Make arrangements with your parents and/or other housemates about what you will do if a disaster occurs.
- Make a first aid kit (see p. 14).
- Make an emergency kit (see p. 49).
- Make a survival kit (see p. 51).
- Make an evacuation plan and rehearse it:
  1. Make sure you know by what routes you can leave the house.
  2. Make sure you know by what ways you can leave the neighbourhood and where the higher places in the area are (for example, make a map of the area showing escape routes).
  3. Make sure you know where the nearest hospitals are.
- Download the Red Cross's first aid app on your phone.

This book explains what to do *during* disasters. You can get the latest news from the radio, television or the Internet.

WHAT TO PAY ATTENTION TO AFTER A DISASTER:

- Make sure that you know where your housemates are.
- Give first aid to those who need it.
- Do not stay in damaged buildings (they could collapse!).
- Leave if you smell gas or fire.
- Stay away from loose electrical wires.
- Inform the emergency services about the locations of victims, gas leaks, fires and electrical wires.
- Let your family know that you are safe through social media.

long-life meals

First-aid kit

Matches

thermal blanket

Medication

hand-cranked flashlight

gas cooker + gas cylinder

hand-cranked radio

batteries

hand-powered charger

mobile phone

water filter

emergency whistle

pan

cash money

copy passports + important papers

bottles of water

important phone numbers

Swiss Army knife

tealights

MAKING AN EMERGENCY KIT

When a disaster occurs, it can take days until emergency services reach you. So always make sure that you have an emergency kit ready with which you can hold out for around 3 days.

Your emergency kit should contain the following:

- a hand-cranked (or battery-powered) radio
- a hand-cranked (or battery-powered) flashlight
- additional batteries if your radio or flashlight are battery-powered
- a hand-powered charger for your mobile phone
- bottles of water: 3 litres per person per day
- long-life meals: at least 1 nourishing meal per person per day
- a water filter that can purify contaminated tap water
- a pan
- a gas cooker and gas cylinder

- a Swiss Army knife
- matches (in waterproof packaging)
- tealights
- an emergency whistle
- thermal blankets: 1 per person
- medication: the daily medication that you and your housemates need, enough for 3 days
- the first-aid kit (see p. 14)
- a list of important phone numbers
- copies of your passports and important papers
- cash money

Matches

emergency blanket

Nylon thread

Water purification tablets

tealights

Full change of clothes

Compass

Swiss Army knife

batteries

hand-cranked Radio

whistle

hand-cranked Flashlight

hand-powered charger Mobile phone

Stainless steel Water bottle

Meal bars

Magnifying glass

Map of the area

First-aid kit

important phone Numbers

pencil

phone

Copy passport + important papers

MAKING A DISASTER SURVIVAL KIT

When a major disaster occurs, you need to be able to act quickly. If you have the following supplies in your house – in a suitcase or backpack, so that you can easily bring them with you – you are prepared for the worst:

- a hand-cranked (or battery-powered) radio
- a hand-cranked (or battery-powered) flashlight
- additional batteries if your radio or flashlight are battery-powered
- a hand-powered charger for your phone
- matches in a waterproof box, or a fire starter
- (several) tealights
- a pencil
- a whistle
- a Swiss Army knife
- water purification tablets
- a stainless steel water bottle (fill it before you leave)

- a number of meal bars
- a long piece of nylon thread
- a magnifying glass (for making fire when the sun is out)
- a map of the area
- a compass
- a full change of clothes
- an emergency blanket
- a list of the most important phone numbers of your family, doctor and emergency services
- copies of your passport and other important papers

Don't forget your phone and first aid kit.

EARTH - EARTHQUAKE

THE WORST The deadliest earthquake ever occurred on 23 January 1556, in Shaanxi, China. Some 830,000 people died. The number of victims was so great because people lived in caves that collapsed during the quake.

- Earthquakes are usually caused by tectonic plates moving alongside or slipping over each other. Due to the melting glaciers and rising sea levels, the pressure on the tectonic plates is changing, resulting in more and more powerful earthquakes.

- Human activity can also cause earthquakes, for example fracking. This is a method of extracting oil or gas from the ground that can cause earth layers to move or sink.

- Around half a million earthquakes occur every year. Of these, around 100,000 can actually be felt, and around 100 of them cause damage. 90 per cent of these earthquakes occurs in the Ring of Fire, which more or less frames the whole Pacific Ocean.

- In 2010, an earthquake in Chili was so powerful that the entire town of Concepción was displaced by 3 metres. It is also in Chili that the strongest quake ever was measured, registering 9.5 on the Richter scale. It happened on 22 May 1960.

- An earthquake near Japan in 2011 (also see the chapter on "Tsunami") caused the rotation of the earth to accelerate. Since then, a day is 1.8 micro-seconds shorter than before.

- In 2015, Mount Everest lost 2.5 centimetres of its height due to an earthquake in Nepal.

WHAT TO DO

IF THE EARTH STARTS TO QUAKE:

- Get down on your hands and knees, so that you can still crawl – but when you crawl, keep one arm over your head as protection.
- Wrap your arms around your head and grab your neck with your hands.
- If there's a table or desk nearby, crawl under it. Curl up into a ball, keeping your head down, and hold on to the table legs.
- No table around? Then keep away as much as you can from things that can fall on top of you. If you're outside, stay away from trees, buildings, cars and other things that can move or collapse.
- Are you in bed? Stay there, turn onto your belly and put a pillow over your head.
- Are you in a cinema or theatre? Remain in your seat, bend forward, wrap your arms around your head and stay seated until the quaking stops.
- Are you on the beach? The earthquake could trigger a tsunami. If a tsunami warning sounds, then move inland and to higher ground as quickly as possible.

EARTH – LANDSLIDE

THE WORST On 16 December 1920, the earth began to move in Haiyuan, China. It became so severe that landslides occurred in 675 places. An area measuring some 20,000 square kilometres was devastated, and more than 100,000 people were killed.

DID YOU KNOW?

- A landslide often occurs after an earthquake, flood, forest fire or volcanic eruption, and is often more destructive than the disaster that caused it.
- There are different types of landslides. If a large section of a rock face breaks off and slides down the mountain, then it's a mountain slide. If it mainly involves loose rocks, then it's called a rock or debris slide. If the slide consists of earth or debris mixed with water, then it's a mud slide.
- An average landslide travels at a speed of 15 kilometres an hour, but it can travel as fast as 55 kilometres an hour. The fastest landslide ever recorded moved at 170 kilometres an hour!
- Landslides are not limited to the planet Earth. There is evidence that they occur in other places in the universe as well, most notably on Mars and Venus.

WHAT TO DO

- Find out whether landslides have occurred in your area before.
- Listen out for strange sounds, like rocks hitting each other or trees breaking.
- If you're by a river, check if the water is turning muddy. Muddy water could indicate a landslide farther upstream.
- Leave the area as soon as you see or hear something suspicious and warn the neighbours. Help people who are not or less mobile to leave the area.
- If you're at home and cannot get away anymore, go to the top floor.
- If you get caught up in a landslide, curl up into a ball and place your arms over your head as protection.
- If, after a landslide, you know where people are stuck, don't go there but tell the rescue workers where they are.

EARTH — AVALANCHE

THE WORST On 31 May 1970, an earthquake in Peru caused an avalanche that defies description. A chunk of ice and snow measuring 910 metres wide and 1,600 metres long came crashing down the mountain of Huascarán at speeds of between 280 and 335 kilometres an hour. More than 17,000 square metres of debris travelled a distance of 18 kilometres, engulfing the towns of Yungay and Ranrahirca under a massive layer of ice, snow, mud and rock. Nearly 20,000 people perished.

DID YOU KNOW?

- An avalanche usually starts when frozen layers of snow beneath a thick blanket of snow break off and start sliding down the slope. That's why the danger of an avalanche is always bigger after a heavy snow storm.
- An avalanche can reach speeds of up to 125 kilometres an hour within 5 seconds, and that speed can reach as high as 400 kilometres an hour.
- Around 150 people are killed by an avalanche every year. In 90 per cent of cases, they (or the people they were with) were responsible for causing the avalanche.

- Once you get caught up in an avalanche, your body quickly sinks down into the snow; a human body is 3 times as heavy as the material that makes up the avalanche.
- As soon as the avalanche comes to a halt, the snow on top freezes within seconds to form a top layer that's as hard as concrete.
- People dug up from under an avalanche within 18 minutes stand a 91 per cent chance of surviving.

WHAT TO DO

- If you decide to go skiing or snowboarding off-piste, make sure you're wearing an avalanche beacon. This device emits a signal if you're trapped under snow, so that rescue workers can find you.
- If you see snow starting to move, move to the side as much as possible: avalanches are heaviest in the middle.
- If the avalanche starts beneath your feet, try to jump up so that you're not dragged along.
- Swim for your life: if the snow gets hold of you, swim along with the flow and try to stay near the surface.
- If you are buried under snow, curl up like a baby, breathe as deeply as possible, and keep your hands by your mouth. As soon as you're still, excavate as much space around you as possible, to increase the amount of oxygen available. Respiration is the main concern: of all fatalities, 90 per cent ran out of oxygen.

57

WATER – FLOODING

THE WORST After 2 years of drought, China was hit by severe rainstorms and melting snow in 1931. During the summer the two major rivers, the Yangtze and the Huai, spilled their banks several times. At a certain point the water levels were 16 metres higher than usual, and 180,000 square kilometres of land were flooded. It is estimated that 4 million people died, while another 50 million people lost all they had.

DID YOU KNOW?

- In case of a flood, it's best to seek higher ground. Still, 95 per cent of people tries to outrun the water.
- Swiftly moving water only needs to reach a depth of 15 centimetres to knock an adult man off his feet.
- A car can float off when the water reaches 60 centimetres. For a small car, 30 centimetres will do.
- There is a chance of floods if rain falls at a rate of more than 2.5 centimetres an hour.
- A "flash flood" is a sudden flood caused by an extreme downpour, or by a dam burst. In that case, you may see a wall of water coming at you that reaches 3 to 6 metres high.
- The chance of flooding at the coast is now 3 to 10 times greater than in the 1960s.

- If the sea level continues to rise at the same pace as now, countries like China, Bangladesh, Vietnam, Japan and India will be hit by massive floods, while 47 per cent of the Dutch population, 6 per cent of the Belgian population, and 4 per cent of the Danish and English population will be threatened by the water.

WHAT TO DO

- Have a battery-powered radio and listen to the news reports.
- If a flood warning is issued, go to higher ground as quickly as possible. Take your pets with you.
- Help people who are less mobile to get away.
- Do not try to walk or drive through swiftly moving water.
- If your car is trapped in water, get out immediately and try to make it to dry ground. Do NOT stay in the car.

- If you cannot get away, then go to the highest place in the house and stay close to a window so that you can crawl onto the roof, if necessary.
- Make sure to have enough long-life food in the house, and bottles of water (a supply for 3 days).
- Fill as many buckets and pans – or the bathtub if you have one – with clean drinking water.
- Disconnect the gas, water and electricity mains before the water pours into the house.
- Cover drains to keep out sewage water.

WATER - TSUNAMI

THE WORST The largest tsunami wave ever measured reached a height of 30 metres and destroyed all trees and vegetation up to 524 metres above the normal water level. It was caused when more than 30 million cubic metres of rock came crashing down into the Lituya Bay of Alaska from a height of almost 1 kilometre. It happened on 9 July 1958.

The deadliest tsunami occurred on 26 December 2004 in the Indian Ocean. An earthquake beneath the floor of the ocean triggered waves that rushed towards land at a speed of 800 kilometres an hour. Across 14 countries, more than 280,000 people died.

DID YOU KNOW?

- The word "tsunami" is a Japanese word composed of "harbour" (*tsu*) and "wave" (*nami*).
- A tsunami can be triggered by an underwater earthquake, by a sudden change in air pressure, by a landslide, or by a volcanic eruption. Or, by the impact of a large meteorite.
- Scientists think that a tsunami, caused by a meteorite impact, destroyed almost all life on earth some 3.5 billion years ago.
- A tsunami does not consist of a single wave, but of a series of waves in succession – referred to as a "wave train".
- A tsunami wave does not curl forwards like a normal wave, but approaches the land like a wall of water.
- The first wave of the tsunami is usually not the highest wave; they successively get higher and more powerful.
- A tsunami can travel as fast as a fighter plane, almost 1,000 kilometres an hour, and it can travel across the ocean for thousands of kilometres before hitting land.
- 80 per cent of tsunamis occurs in the so-called Ring of Fire, which more or less frames the whole Pacific Ocean.

WHAT TO DO

- Have a battery-powered radio and listen to the news reports.
- If you are in a coastal area and feel an earthquake, head for higher ground as a precaution.
- If you see the seawater suddenly withdraw from the beach, head for higher ground as quickly as you can and as far inland as possible.
- Flee on foot if you can – cars often get stuck in congestion, which leaves you trapped.
- Do not return home after the first few waves. More waves may be on their way.
- Don't linger to look. If you can see a tsunami wave approaching, it's too late to escape.
- If you are swept away by a tsunami, do not try to swim. Try instead to grab onto something that floats, and let yourself float along with the wave.

THE WORST In 1769, lightning struck the church of San Nazaro in Brescia, in the Republic of Venice. The church served as a storage depot for 90,000 kilos of gunpowder. The ensuing explosion destroyed one-sixth of the city and killed 9,000 people.

DID YOU KNOW?

- Astraphobia means fear of thunder and lightning. Are you only afraid of thunder? Then you are afflicted by brontophobia.
- To calculate the distance between you and a thunderstorm, count the number of seconds between the flash of lightning and the crack of thunder, and divide by 3. That gives you the approximate number of kilometres between you and the storm.
- The lightning flash causes the surrounding air to heat up so quickly that it does so with a bang – that's the sound of thunder. The air can reach temperatures of up to 10,000 degrees Celsius.
- Around the world, there are approximately 1,800 thunderstorms taking place at every moment of the day. That adds up to 16 million thunderstorms a year.
- People who are struck by lightning often suffer strange, branch-shaped burns on their body, known as Lichtenberg figures.
- Every year, worldwide, an estimated 264,000 people are struck by lightning, with 24,000 fatalities.
- Every day, lightning strikes the earth around 10,000 times. Of every 10 strikes, 1 to 2 causes a fire.

- Roy Sullivan was struck by lightning 7 times: in his garden, in his car, while out fishing, even inside his home. But he survived them all.

WHAT TO DO

- Go inside as soon as you hear thunder.
- Close doors and windows, and keep away from windows.
- Switch off all devices with an electric plug, such as the television and desktop computer.
- Do not take a shower or a bath or use the landline telephone during a thunderstorm. If lightning strikes, you could be electrocuted.
- If you cannot shelter inside a building, then head for lower ground. Never hide under a tree or in the vicinity of water or metal.
- If you're in a car during a thunderstorm, then stay where you are.
- If someone is struck by lightning and stops breathing, **call the emergency telephone number.** Immediately attempt to resuscitate the victim (see p. 12) until the ambulance arrives.
- There is no danger in touching people after they've been struck by lightning.

ATMOSPHERE – SNOWSTORM

THE WORST The worst snow storm in history occurred in Iran, from 3 to 8 February 1972. The storm covered part of the country with a layer of snow that reached 8 metres in places. Some 170,000 square kilometres were buried under snow for 1 whole week. 200 villages disappeared, and 4,000 people perished.

WHAT TO DO

- Have a battery-powered radio and listen to the news reports.
- Stay indoors. There might be a power cut.
- Wear loose, light clothing – many layers on top of each other.
- Make sure all pets are inside.
- Open the tap to a slight trickle, to prevent the mains from freezing.
- Do not set the heating to a lower temperature overnight.
- If you get caught up in a snow storm outdoors, see to it that you eat and drink sufficiently. Don't consume snow, as this will cool you down. Keep moving, and try to stay out of the wind.
- If you absolutely have to drive a car through a snow storm, always pack the following: warm clothing, water, food, blankets, jumper cables, fully charged mobile telephones, rope and tealights.

▶ Also read the chapter on "Hypothermia".

DID YOU KNOW?

- If snow falls in combination with wind force 6 or 7, then this is termed a snow storm. With wind force 8, it is termed a blizzard. When snow blows up from the ground, it is termed a ground blizzard.
- In a blizzard, the wind can be as forceful as during a hurricane.
- A severe snow storm can drop as much as 39 billion kilos of snow. Such a storm contains as much energy as 120 atomic bombs.
- The longest-lasting snow storm on earth is in Antarctica – it simply never stops.
- An American city, Syracuse, was so fed up with snow that the municipality declared snowfall before Christmas illegal. It didn't help.
- Snowflakes seem white but are actually devoid of colour. We see them as white because of the light that reflects off them.
- The largest snowflake ever recorded measured 38 centimetres in diametre and 20 centimetres in width. It fell in Montana, USA, in 1887.

ATMOSPHERE - HEAT WAVE

THE WORST You might think that the worst heat waves occur in hot countries, but one of the worst heat waves occurred in Europe in 2003. That summer more than 70,000 people died because of the heat, mainly elderly people.

France was hit hardest. They were not used to such temperatures (in August of that year it was more than 40 degrees Celsius for 8 days in a row), and most buildings didn't have air-conditioning. So many people died in that period that the undertakers in Paris used a refrigerated warehouse to store the victims until they could be identified.

DID YOU KNOW?

- A heat wave is usually the result of a high pressure area remaining in one spot for a prolonged period of time. The high pressure prevents heat from rising up from the earth's surface. And if hot air does not rise up, rain won't form, and the air will only get hotter.
- In the Netherlands and Belgium, a heat wave is defined as 5 consecutive days of temperatures in excess of 25 degrees Celsius, with 3 days reaching temperatures above 30 degrees.
- The third day of a heat wave is the most dangerous day: that's when people who have trouble coping with heat start to develop complaints.
- During a heat wave, it's usually hotter in the city than in the countryside. That's because of the "urban heat island effect": buildings and roads absorb the solar energy, adding heat to the area.
- Plants generally filter all sorts of substances from the air that are bad for us, such as ozone. But if conditions become very hot, then the plants close their pores to retain moisture, and no longer perform their filtering function. As a result you might have trouble breathing and your eyes might start to sting.

WHAT TO DO

- Wear light-coloured loose clothing. Dark clothing absorbs the heat.
- Drink 2 to 3 litres of water a day, even if you're not thirsty.
- Do not eat large portions, but smaller portions more frequently throughout the day.
- No air-conditioning or a fan at home? Then it's best to spend the hottest part of the day, between 12 and 4 in the afternoon, in large buildings, which are often cooler.
- Do everything a bit more slowly than usual. Do not engage in sports or exercise. If you really need to go out, then cover your head and stick to the shade as much as you can.
- Close the curtains of windows that catch the sun. It is cooler inside than outside? Then keep the windows closed. But if it's warmer inside than outside, then open the windows wide.
- Never stay inside a hot car and don't leave your pet in the car either.
- Do not go from extreme heat outside to extreme cold inside, or vice versa.
- Look after the people and animals in your vicinity. Make sure that elderly people, small children and overweight people get enough to drink – but no alcohol, as alcohol withdraws water from your body.

ATMOSPHERE – DROUGHT

THE WORST From 1876 to 1878, the lack of rain in both China and India caused massive famines. Between 9 and 13 million people died in China, and 5 million died in India.

DID YOU KNOW?

- There are 4 types of drought:
  1. METEOROLOGICAL DROUGHT (lack of rain);
  2. AGRARIAN DROUGHT (lack of moisture in the ground);
  3. HYDROLOGICAL DROUGHT (low water levels in lakes and reservoirs);
  4. SOCIO-ECONOMIC DROUGHT (lack of drinking water and flowing water).
- An important cause of prolonged drought is the phenomenon known as El Niño: due to the heating up of the oceans, humid air is displaced to areas where it always rains a lot, while no rains fall in the areas that need it most.
- Most droughts occur in Africa – especially in the Horn of Africa – and in Afghanistan, China, India, Iran and Morocco.
- More and longer droughts are expected to occur as a result of climate change.
- Different types of food crops require different amounts of water to grow: a single walnut requires over 18 litres of water, half a kilo of potatoes requires 125 litres, half a kilo of rice requires 1700 litres, and half a kilo of beef requires 6800 litres.
- Just 0.003 per cent of water on earth is drinkable.

WHAT TO DO

- Never throw water away, but use it for instance to water plants.
- Always repair a leaking tap.
- Cut your shower time to a minimum and never let a tap run unnecessarily (e.g. when brushing your teeth).
- You can put a bucket of water next to you while showering to collect water for plants.
- Do the dishes in a tub of water, rather than under a running tap.
- Don't use the dish washer and laundry machine until they are completely full.

ATMOSPHERE – TORNADO

THE WORST On 26 April 1989, a tornado occurred in Manikganj, Bangladesh. Named after the cities it hit, the Daulatpur-Saturia tornado stretched 1.5 kilometres wide and travelled no less than 80 kilometres across land. It killed around 1300 people, injured another 12,000 people, and left 80,000 people homeless. Approximately half of the world's fatalities due to tornados happen in Bangladesh.

- A tornado is a whirlwind that develops over land. It is generally not wider than 500 metres and often travels no farther than 20 kilometres.
- A tornado over water is called a waterspout. Although a tornado wind generally doesn't spin faster than 160 kilometres an hour, it can reach speeds of up to 480 kilometres an hour.
- Tornados can occur everywhere on earth.
- Most (and the strongest) tornados occur in the United States: on average, 1274 a year. The areas where they occur most frequently – at the centre of the continent – is known as Tornado Alley.
- Most tornados develop between 3 in the afternoon and 9 in the evening.
- A 19-year-old boy named Matt Suter was sucked out of a mobile home and dropped nearly 400 metres away in a field. He suffered only minor injuries.
- In the southern hemisphere, a tornado usually spins clockwise, and in the northern hemisphere, usually anti-clockwise.
- Some tornados are invisible; you can only see them if they pick up sand, dust or other objects.

WHAT TO DO
IF A TORNADO APPROACHES:

- Have a battery-powered radio and listen to the news reports.
- Do not wait until you can see the tornado.
- Shelter in the cellar if you can, or else in a room or corridor without windows, on the lowest floor of the building. Take your pets with you.
- Keep away from heavy furniture or things that might fall on your head.
- Curl up into a ball, with your head facing the wall and your arms wrapped around your head and neck for protection.
- If you're outside, then find the lowest possible spot (a ditch, a hole in the ground), and lie down flat with your arms covering your head.
- Camper vans, mobile homes and cars are not a safe shelter. But if you can't get away, then curl up into a ball beneath the level of windows and cover your head with your arms and if possible with a blanket as well.

ATMOSPHERE – HURRICANE

THE WORST On 8 November 1970, a hurricane developed in the Bay of Bengal that hit land in East Pakistan (now Bangladesh) with wind speeds of up to 185 kilometres an hour. The hurricane created a storm surge that was responsible for most fatalities. All in all, cyclone Bhola (as it was named) killed some 500,000 people.

DID YOU KNOW?

- A hurricane is a tropical storm that develops over sea.
- The eye of the hurricane – at the centre of the storm, which is calm – usually has a diametre of between 30 and 50 kilometres. Around this eye, a storm revolves with wind speeds of between 120 and 250 kilometres an hour.
- A hurricane can be hundreds of kilometres wide.
- Hurricanes only occur in areas between the eighth and fifteenth latitude to the north and south of the equator.
- Since 1953, all hurricanes are given a name. These names begin with an "a" at the start of the year, and progress through the alphabet as the year proceeds. Until 1978, hurricanes were only given female names.
- Names can be reused every 6 years, but if a hurricane was particularly destructive, such as Katrina, Mitch, Sandy and Andrew, then this name can no longer be reused and is removed from the list.
- Hurricanes are called typhoons if they occur in the Pacific Ocean and cyclones if they occur in the Indian Ocean.
- The hurricane season runs from mid-May to the end of November.
- A hurricane is the most destructive natural phenomenon. On average, hurricanes kill 10,000 people each year.
- According to the NASA, the number of hurricanes averages 85 a year, but many of these never reach land.
- A hurricane larger than the planet earth has been happening on planet Jupiter for over 300 years.
- Climate change is likely to cause more and more powerful hurricanes.

WHAT TO DO

- Have a battery-powered radio and listen to the news reports.
- Take everything indoors that could blow away. Also bring the pets inside.
- Close all doors and windows, close the shutters or board up the windows from the outside.
- Make sure to have enough long-life food and bottles of water in the house (for 3 days).
- Keep a torch and batteries within reach in case there's a power cut.
- If the hurricane hits your house: stay away from windows and from objects that might fall. Lie down flat under a table, if possible.
- Never take shelter in a camper van, mobile home or car.
- Do not leave the house until it has been confirmed that it is safe to do so. At the eye of the hurricane all is quiet and seemingly safe, but it won't be long before the other side hits!

FIRE - CITY FIRE

THE WORST On 1 September 1923, just when people were preparing lunch over a fire, an earthquake occurred in Tokyo, Japan. The many small fires quickly caused large fires to break out, all across the city. Some turned into a firestorm and even caused a fire tornado. The heat was such that the asphalt melted, trapping people who were then burnt alive. Most of the fatalities following the earthquake were caused by the fires.

DID YOU KNOW?

- Fire always consists of 3 elements: fuel, oxygen and heat. Take away any one of these 3, and fire is impossible.
- Burning fires only occur on earth. There isn't enough oxygen elsewhere in the universe.
- The more oxygen reaches a fire, the hotter it gets.
- You can usually tell how hot a fire is by the colour of the flames: the heat displays the same colours as the rainbow. Red is the "coolest" (500-800 degrees Celsius), violet-white is the hottest (over 1,600 degrees Celsius). Carbon subnitride can cause the hottest flame of all: 4,987 degrees Celsius.
- Most domestic fires are the result of cooking activities in the kitchen.
- Most fatalities of domestic fires are the result of cigarette-induced fires (for instance when smoking in bed).
- Around 265,000 people die of burns each year.
- This book (and other paper) will ignite spontaneously under conditions of 233 degrees Celsius heat.
- No one knows who invented the hydrant. The patent was lost... in a fire!
- In 1900, firefighting was an Olympic sport.

- Go outside and call the emergency telephone number, taking other people with you.
- Do not use a lift, but take the stairs.
- Smoke rises up, so it's best to stay as low as you can (crawl across the floor) if the room fills up with smoke. Close doors and windows as you pass through them.
- If a door feels hot, then a fire could be raging on the other side. Do not open it but look for another way out.

IF YOU CANNOT LEAVE THE ROOM BECAUSE OF THE FLAMES:
- Keep the door shut.
- **Phone the emergency telephone number.**
- Use a wet towel to block the crack under the door.
- Open the window and try to attract people's attention.

IF YOUR CLOTHES CATCH FIRE:
- Stop moving about. The flames will grow bigger if you run.
- Lie down on the ground and roll back and forth to extinguish the flames.
- Douse your clothes with water, jump into a pond or ditch if possible! Or use a fire blanket to smother the flames.

▶ Also read the chapter on "Burns".

WHAT TO DO
BEFORE A FIRE OCCURS:
- Mount a smoke alarm in your home.
- Have a fire extinguisher and/or fire blanket in your home.
- Figure out the best escape routes.
- Arrange an assembly spot with your housemates.

IF THERE'S A FIRE:
- Shout "Fire!" as loudly as you can, if there are other people in the house.

FIRE – WILDFIRE

THE WORST The weather was dry throughout the summer of 1871, and everyone in the town of Peshtigo (Wisconsin, USA) had become used to the smell of small fires. Perhaps that's why people were caught completely by surprise when, on 8 October, a wall of fire came bearing down on them. The fire reached 1.5 kilometres high, stretched 8 kilometres wide, reached temperatures of over 1,000 degrees Celsius and travelled at a speed of 150 kilometres an hour. The fire was so hot that people who jumped into the river were boiled alive. Over 5,000 square kilometres of land was destroyed and 2,500 people died.

DID YOU KNOW?

- Every year, between 50,000 and 100,000 wildfires occur worldwide.
- Every year, around 3.5 million square kilometres of nature goes up in smoke.
- There are 3 types of wildfire:
  1. GROUND FIRE: fire in the subterranean layer;
  2. BRUSHFIRE: fire in the undergrowth (grass, shrubs, bushes);
  3. CROWN FIRE: fire in the tree tops;
- More than 80 per cent of wildfires is caused by humans, for instance by a cigarette butt or a campfire that wasn't fully extinguished.
- In Australia, no less than 50 per cent of wildfires is caused deliberately or "under suspicious circumstances".
- Lightning is an important cause of wildfire: of every 100,000 lightning strikes every day, 10 to 20 per cent causes a wildfire (large or small).
- Forest fires travel faster uphill than downhill.
- Climate change is expected to cause more wildfires, especially in Australia, Europe and North America.

WHAT TO DO

IF YOU SEE SMOKE IN A NATURAL AREA:

- **Phone the emergency telephone number.**
- Start moving in the opposite direction as quickly as possible.
- Warn all the people you see and ring the bells of nearby houses.

IS A WILDFIRE APPROACHING YOUR HOME?

- Have a battery-powered radio and listen to news reports to find out if you need to evacuate.
- Bring your pets inside.
- Close all doors and windows to keep out the smoke.
- Make sure you know where everyone in the house is, so that you can leave quickly if necessary. Arrange an assembly point with your housemates.
- Are you in a car? Then set the air-conditioning to the recirculation mode, not to the fresh air mode.

FIRE – VOLCANIC ERUPTION

THE WORST The worst recorded volcanic eruption occurred in 1815, on the Indonesian island of Sumbawa. The eruption of the Tambora volcano on 10 April pushed the island several metres above sea level in places. The kingdom of Tambora was buried under a layer of ash of 1.5 to 10 metres deep. The eruption and the tsunami that followed killed 92,000 people.

Due to all the ash that ended up in the stratosphere, the earth was shielded from the sun's rays, preventing a summer season the next year. As a result the harvests failed, and probably another 100,000 people died of starvation.

DID YOU KNOW?

- A volcano is a place where the earth's surface has an open connection to the molten rock beneath, at a depth of around 30 kilometres. While inside the earth, this molten rock is called magma. When the volcano erupts and the magma comes pouring out, it is called lava.
- The word "volcano" comes from the Latin word "vulcanus", which means "burning mountain".
- A volcano can emerge very quickly: the Mexican volcano Paricutín emerged in just 1 night, and within a week it was already 100 metres high.
- The ashes of a volcano contain various poisonous substances and can cause breathing difficulties, eye complaints and lung disease.
- When a volcano erupts, it not only spews forth lava and ashes but can also cause earthquakes, tsunamis, floods, landslides and mudslides.
- There are at least 1,500 active volcanos worldwide. At every minute of the day around 20 are actively erupting, three-quarters of which are under the sea.

- Lava has a temperature of between 700 and 1,600 degrees Celsius.
- Volcanic pumice is the only type of rock that can float.
- Super volcanos erupt just once in 100,000 years or so, but they can cause an ice age because the vast amounts of ash in the stratosphere can block out the sun.

WHAT TO DO

IF YOU LIVE NEAR AN ACTIVE VOLCANO:

- Always have a survival kit fully stocked and ready to use (see p. 51).
- Know how to get away as fast as possible in case you need to evacuate.

DURING AN ERUPTION:

- Have a battery-powered radio and listen to the news reports to find out if you need to evacuate.
- Close all doors and windows.
- Cover your mouth and nose with a mask or cloth, to avoid breathing in ashes.
- If you're outside: head for higher ground and protect your head and eyes against ashes and falling stones.
- As soon as the ash rain stops: remove the ashes wherever it fell, also from plants.
- Wash everything in your surroundings, to avoid breathing in or ingesting any ashes.

PEOPLE – ATTACK

THE WORST In 1793, the revolutionary politician Robespierre came to power in France. Within just a few months, 40,000 people who were opposed to the revolutionary regime were killed – at least 16,594 were decapitated by the guillotine.

An English reporter described Robespierre's actions as "terrorism", and the French government as "terrorists". We still use these words today for people who try to get their way by sowing fear.

DID YOU KNOW?

- The panic caused by an attack often causes more damage than the attack itself. After the attack on the World Trade Center in New York in 2001, many people were afraid to travel by air and took the car instead. This led to more deaths in traffic accidents than the number of victims killed by the WTC attack.
- Most attacks take place in non-western countries. The top-10 of countries in terms of number of attacks are – in decreasing order – Iraq, Pakistan, Afghanistan, India, Nigeria, Somalia, Yemen, Syria, Sri Lanka and Thailand.
- Just 2.6 per cent of deaths due to an attack occurs in the West.
- Most attacks in western countries are committed by people born and raised there. 90 per cent of these attacks is committed by just 1 or 2 people, rather than by groups. And most of the perpetrators – no less than 67 per cent – are not motivated by religion but by politics. One example is Anders Breivik, who killed 77 people in Norway in 2011, in an attempt to bring about the downfall of the Labour party.
- The chance of being killed by an attack is 1 in 20 million. That means you have just as much chance of being killed by a piece of furniture falling on your head.

WHAT TO DO

IF YOU SEE PEOPLE APPROACHING WITH WEAPONS:

- If you can run away, do so as fast as you can. It's better than lying down flat on the ground.
- Leave all your belongings behind, so that you can move as fast as possible.
- Are you in another room? Then barricade the door and switch your mobile phone to silent mode. Turn off the lights.

- Try to shelter behind a solid wall – so not behind a door or window that bullets can easily penetrate.
- Don't try to see whether the attacker is still around. If you can see him, then he can see you.
- If you can: **call the emergency telephone number** and say where you are, how many attackers there are, and what weapons they are carrying.
- If you managed to leave the building, warn everyone you see.

PEOPLE – NUCLEAR DISASTER

THE WORST On 26 April 1986, a nuclear plant in Chernobyl, Ukraine, exploded. The radioactive cloud contaminated an area of 100,000 square kilometres – home to a population of 5 million people. The amount of radiation released was 100 times the radiation released by the 2 atomic bombs dropped on Japan in 1945. Radioactive fallout was registered as far away as Wales, Great Britain. The actual explosion killed less than 100 people, but the radiation continues to have an impact until today. People are still dying of thyroid cancer caused by this nuclear disaster, and after 30 years, one-tenth of all wild boars in Germany are still too radioactive to be fit for consumption.

DID YOU KNOW?

- Nuclear technology is used in a wide variety of institutes: in hospitals, at universities and in scientific research institutes, in almost every form of industry (from food to weapons), and of course in nuclear power plants.
- The 2 atomic bombs that the United States dropped on Japan in 1945 caused the first nuclear disaster and claimed 200,000 lives.
- Nuclear radiation has an effect on DNA. After Chernobyl, twice as many children were born with some form of defect. Such defects have also been found among all sorts of animal species.
- There are currently more than 400 nuclear power plants across the world that produce 6 per cent of the power and 14 per cent of the electricity produced worldwide.
- After a nuclear disaster, you can rid yourself of 90 per cent of radioactive particles by removing your clothes.
- Lake Karachay in Russia was used as a dumping ground for radioactive waste. It is the most contaminated place on earth: standing on the edge of the lake for 1 hour is enough to absorb a lethal dose of radiation.
- Tobacco contains polonium-210, so someone who smokes a pack of cigarettes a day absorbs as much radiation per year as having 200 x-rays taken of his lungs.
- A proper solution for radioactive waste has still to be found.

WHAT TO DO

- Make sure to always have an emergency kit stocked up and ready to use (see p. 49).
- Go inside, take your pets with you, close all doors and windows and switch off the air-conditioning.
- If possible, stay in a room without windows.
- Have a battery-powered radio and listen to the news reports.
- If possible, keep a mobile phone at hand with a hand-powered charger.
- Stay indoors for as long as possible.

PEOPLE – INDUSTRIAL DISASTER

THE WORST In the night of 3 December 1984, the Union Carbide plant in Bhopal, India, where chemical pesticides were made, released a cloud of poison, immediately killing 3,787 people and injuring nearly 560,000. In the following months, another 12,000 deaths were reported. But the disaster didn't end there: until today, people continue to fall sick and die due to respiratory infections, heart failure and cancer. Now, a third generation of children is being born with severe mental and physical defects.

DID YOU KNOW?

- Industrial disasters can take various forms: from explosions to leaks at factories and the (illegal) dumping of industrial waste to oil spills, the plastic pollution of the oceans and the use of chemical weapons.
- Fortunately, the number of oil leaks from tankers has decreased sharply. Last year, just 8 million litres leaked from tankers; in the 1970s that figure was, on average, 312 million litres a year.
- Three-quarters of industrial disasters occur in Asia. An industrial disaster happens almost daily in China. This isn't just due to the working conditions there, but also because the West outsources the most hazardous jobs mainly to China.
- Every year, the global industry is responsible for releasing 10 billion kilos of toxic chemical substances into nature. 2 billion kilos of these substances are proven to cause cancer.
- Every year, all of us together throw out 400 billion kilos of hazardous waste.
- The world's largest electronic waste belt is in Guiyu, China. 88 per cent of the children there suffers from lead poisoning.
- Every year, 5.5 million die as a result of air pollution.
- The use of pesticides is responsible for 220,000 deaths each year.

WHAT TO DO

IF A TOXIC CLOUD IS COMING YOUR WAY:

- Make sure to always have an emergency kit stocked and ready to use (see p. 49).
- Go inside and take your pets with you.
- Close all doors and windows, switch off the air-conditioning, and close all ventilation slits.
- Have a battery-powered radio and listen to the news reports.
- Do not make open fire and do not let anyone smoke.

LOOK AFTER YOUR ENVIRONMENT:

- Produce as little waste as you can.
- Get rid of waste properly.

PEOPLE - WAR

THE WORST The Second World War claimed the greatest number of lives: between 40 and 72 million. More than 30 countries participated and more than 100 million soldiers were deployed to the various fronts.

DID YOU KNOW?

- Since 3600 B.C., some 14,000 large wars have killed some 4 billion people.
- The shortest war in history lasted 38 minutes. That's how quickly Zanzibar surrendered to Great Britain in 1896.
- In the past 3,400 years, peace has reigned across the whole planet for just 268 years.
- Most wars have been conducted for economic reasons: to acquire greater wealth. Other important reasons have been religion, a desire for revenge, and to conquer territory.
- Very many countries are involved in a war either directly or indirectly. In 2017, for example, just 10 countries worldwide were not involved in a war in some way.
- Out of every 122 people worldwide, 1 person is fleeing war or persecution. That makes 42,500 new refugees every day.
- Half of all refugees are children.
- Wars continue to claim lives after the cessation of hostilities. There are still 110 million landmines scattered around the globe, killing or injuring a person every 15 minutes.
- At least 250,000 child soldiers are involved in a war, somewhere in the world.

WHAT TO DO

- Listen to the radio and do what the authorities tell you to do. Do not listen to rumours.
- Help your parents make your house as self-sufficient as possible. You could install solar cells, for example, to make sure you still have power if the electricity or gas supply is cut.
- Make sure to have an emergency kit stocked and ready to use (see p. 49).
- Carefully read the chapters on "Nuclear disaster" (in case an atomic weapon is used) and on "Attack".
- Try to carry on with life as normally as possible.

PEOPLE – EPIDEMICS

THE WORST Between the year 541 and 542, the Justinian Plague killed 100 million people– almost half of the world's population at the time. A form of bubonic plague, the disease was transmitted by the fleas carried by rats. The disease started in Egypt but was spread around the world by the rats on board ships.

People blamed the Roman emperor Justinian for the outbreak, saying that he was being punished by God – and that he was perhaps the devil himself. That's why they called it the Justinian Plague. It took 225 years for the world to be rid of the disease.

DID YOU KNOW?

- An epidemic is an infectious or viral disease that spreads quickly among a large number of people within a certain geographical region. Once an epidemic travels beyond this certain region it's called a pandemic.

- Between 1346 and 1350, the plague known as Black Death managed to kill approximately 50 million people: 60 per cent of Europe's population was wiped out.
- The first official pandemic occurred in 1918: the Spanish flu. It killed 75 million people.

- A most unusual epidemic occurred in 1962, in what was then called Tanganyika (now Tanzania). Children at a school started laughing and couldn't stop – and they infected other children. In the end, 14 schools had to close down and 1,000 children couldn't stop laughing. The shortest spell of laughter lasted a number of hours, the longest lasted 16 days. Eventually the epidemic died away.
- The most common form of epidemic is the flu. Every year the world is afflicted by various forms of the flu, claiming between 250,000 and 500,000 lives.

WHAT TO DO

- Listen to the radio to understand the type of epidemic.
- Make sure to have enough food and drink in the house in case you get sick.
- Think of people in your vicinity who might be alone and in need of help.
- If the disease is transmitted by air, be sure to wear a mouth mask.
- Do not get too close to people who are sick.
- If you're sick, it's better to stay home and not to go to school, shops or work.
- Cover your mouth when coughing, and mouth and nose when sneezing.
- Touch your eyes, nose and mouth as little as possible.
- Wash your hands regularly using antibacterial soap.
- Get enough sleep and exercise, and eat healthy foods.

Far-away DISASTERS

WHAT CAN YOU DO?

We see it on our screens and read about it in newspapers: war, famine, floods, refugees and many more disasters. The disaster might be happening on the other side of the globe – but there's still a lot we can do.

Here are a few examples (and you can probably think of others besides):

COLLECT MONEY

Whenever a disaster occurs, the people affected always need money to help them rebuild their lives. You can collect money in all sorts of ways, but it's probably most effective to do it together with your friends, your class or sports club, or perhaps with the whole school. You could organise:

- a flea market where people can sell the stuff they no longer need or use at home;
- a sports event, in which people can sponsor the participants for every round they run, every dance on the floor, every point your team scores, and so on;
- a street sale of home-made cookies and cakes;
- an art fair where people can sell their own creative products: cards, paintings, candles, notebooks, and so on;
- doing odd jobs around the neighbourhood in return for a donation;
- a lottery or auction or raffle (you could use part of the money raised as prize money);
- a car-wash service at the school parking grounds;
- a performance – theatre, music, storytelling – where the admission fees are donated.

Tip: see if you can work with local radio or television broadcasters, and use the Internet. Make people aware of the campaign via Facebook, Twitter, Instagram or any other media, and ask them to help you help others.

COLLECT GOODS

People who have lost their homes often need a lot of goods. You can help collect such goods. But before you begin, find out what goods are required and where you can deliver them.

- Make a flyer telling people what goods are required and on what day you'll pass by to collect them. Spread the flyers from door to door. You can also work with a shop or school in the neighbourhood, and arrange that people can drop off goods there until a certain date.
- Food: talk to the local supermarkets to organise a collection of canned food. People can brings cans from home or buy and donate them on the spot.
- Clothing: find out what the weather conditions are in the affected region and organise a clothing collection.

HELP REFUGEES IN YOUR NEIGHBOURHOOD

Help refugees feel welcome in your neighbourhood. You could bring them things for their children, for example: put some toys or drawing materials in a box and make it look nice. Or offer your services as a volunteer.

ADOPT A SCHOOL

Ask your teacher whether your school can adopt a school in the disaster area. Then you can organise markets (or other happenings, see above) to raise money for that school.

Students at the 2 schools can also write to each other. In this way you are helping other people and making friends on the other side of the world, at the same time.

Never forget: you can make a difference on your own!
(And doing it with others will amplify the difference.)

The following international organisations offer relief in case of disasters:

- The Red Cross – WWW.ICRC.ORG
- Doctors without Borders – WWW.DOCTORSWITHOUTBORDERS.ORG
- Unicef – WWW.UNICEF.ORG
- UNHCR – WWW.UNHCR.ORG